The English Disease

Richard Boden

First published in 2016 by **red hand books**
trading name of Red Hand Media Ltd
Flexadux House, Grange Road
Gainsborough DN21 1QB

www.redhandbooks.co.uk

This edition: ISBN 978-1-910346-16-7

A CIP catalogue record for this book is available from the British Library

Prepared for publication by red hand books
Cover design: James Castleden

The English Disease

Richard Boden

For Mum and Dad,
Sarah, Joe and Grace

Acknowledgements are due to the following, where some of these poems first appeared: Acumen, Poetry Ealing, The Rialto, Seam, Smiths Knoll, South, Staple

Contents

Part One

Part Two At Vauxhall - A Tour of the Gardens in Their Heyday

Part One

FIGHTING OFF THE GIRLS

Let me say this happened only once,
some time after our sex education –
that stiff talk and slide-show in the dark,
our eyes widening with vocabulary –

when I came out blinking and converted,
to spend the next two weeks at home
pleading silently with my parents
not to ask me to ask them any questions.

I used to catch myself watching them doing the garden,
shocked at myself, imagining them
naked, hairy, and worst of all,
cheerful, wiggling the seedlings into the earth.

Night after night, I saw myself closing my eyes
and kissing the mirror. Girls. One by one,
I would kiss them and wonder, tracing the creases
and curves. If only I'd let myself let them...

That summer the school field seemed bigger than ever.
I knew they'd be waiting.
I had studied their movements.
I knew that at least five or six of them loved me.

That's why I played along, so that when they caught me,
I would simply pretend that it hurt;
pretend, that is, till they panted and triumphed
above me, crushing me, making me panic –

what would they do to me? which of the diagrams?
Only after the bell, did I find myself
slowly getting to my feet,
rubbing at the grass stains.

NEAP-FEVER

It's been happening for hours. How much
longer can they keep this up? The wind has dropped;
exhausted bunting flags. The whole town's gone quiet
at last.

The predictions are perfect: it promises to be
the lowest incoming tide ever seen!
The traditional excitements are jealously
guarded.

They suspect each horizon in turn.
Everyone knows a good neap means business:
the backwater must not be
disturbed.

Alone in his apartment inland,
the nervous, outgoing Mayor
is going over and over
his lines.

It can't be long now. In a minute,
the special reporter will whisper his
'This is incredible! Nothing is actually happening!'
worldwide.

Down at the harbour, silt licks silt.
Three-quarters of the moon toils through the sky.
The air of expectation grows
stagnant.

After the speech, not a dry eye can be heard.
The ceremonial handkerchiefs are flourished and wiped.
Ever so slowly, the Golden Rule is
applied.

A ripple. Some hush. All England inspects.
When it's over, they emerge from the shallows.
People are waiting. Lives go by. No, just below
average.

A REPOSSESSION

My eyes never did adjust
to that sullenness of rooms,
walls bared, the sense of something
vicious, cornered. I kept

expecting a gusting wind,
some mad crescendo. Only
snake's-head flex lolling from ceilings;
wrenched, astonished plumbing;

the tang of damp instead.
The paradigm of home
beached, gutted, boned.
Even the agent lost for words,

reduced to measurements.
And on the back bedroom door,
a hand-drawn height chart,
hurriedly abandoned, stunted.

MY SON, THE FIRST DOG IN SPACE

Nor, I might add, was it easy
looking on, obedient with concern,
shuddering to think of the countdown
to the shuddering wrench of the launch,
when, all at once, he was lifted clear –

clear of all the trepidation,
all the safety checks and consultations,
the wizardry and acumen,
the hopes and hitches that went into him
from the night of his conception.

Now as he travels further out
in his lone trajectory, what is it
in me that makes me need to interpret
every yelp and snuffle and whine
as joy unleashed, as he aims for the dark,

ever-expanding heart of whatever lies ahead?

COSTUMES

Behind the curtain, in the dark,
the old school productions
we'd come to sort out
lurked: when we triggered the locks,

dank groaned, re-opened. We gasped.
What had we unearthed? A loam
of buried shirts; the rancid trove
of first-night nerves and ill-rehearsed

moves, stiff with emotion; discontinued
lines; wrong sizes crushed and mortified.
All those adolescent performances
transformed by age! We bravely unpicked

each scene. Not a single character
worth keeping. Time for a final
catharsis: we plunged our hands in.
Like rival magicians who pluck at

silk after silk up their sleeves,
snuffing the flames, faster and faster,
more and more deftly, we ransacked whole shows,
plundering the dialogues,

flinging out the choruses –
hundreds of sequins bursting the air! –
feeling the soliloquies
of other, more serious years.

'Why do you dress me in burrowed robes?'
Epaulette-silly, clutching my heart,
I swaggered with each uniform, a tragic
cast-off king. Name-tags gathered in heaps.

For once, we could have been anyone;
we must have tried everything.
So which particular movement or speech
made me turn and see you weren't acting

any more, were simply staring at me,
I don't quite know. Nor, in the now
altering and fitting light, exactly
what made me long to fall to my knees

and believe in us, my *déesse*
ex machina, my queen, my natural;
at least until I glanced away
afraid that someone might come in.

BATHING GRANDMA

Only Mum could do it.
The rest of us, all male,
shrank to hear her lowered,
quailing, into steam,

her kettled hell.
We just did as we were told,
glad not to stare
at the tiny, bird-like cries

wrung from her, as she
fought the scalding and
flinched towards the enamel.
Quiet's sudden plunge.

*

Soon, we'd imagine her naked,
grey, umbilical; my idea
of a boiled potato;
vulcanized junket; an emergent

behemoth, dripping her scales...
Our bad mouths stopped at her navel:
below was beyond us,
out of our depth, out of our neat

little minds... And then we were
older and over it, used to
Mum's accomplishment,
ritually bored, chain-bored.

*

All along, Dad is useless
in the kitchen, wearing
oven gloves. We fiddle
with our knives. In twenty years,

friends will see the likenesses,
but now, in time for dinner,
Grandma – rinsed and dusted,
brighter, pinker – is delivered.

We move the furniture for her.
Mum's amazing, midwife's hands
still wiping, find an apron:
Sunday starts; we may begin.

RUMPELSTILTSKIN

i *The Queen*

If not, it was a certain, lingering death.
And I was desperate at the time, reduced to
prayer, unable to believe in much,
least of all in a saviour, and least of all

my eyes, when he appeared. I flinched. Of course,
what had sprung to mind was no ordinary hero,
but nothing – or rather no one – like this.
What was he? What was this stunted pop-up,

this textbook horrid? There were no introductions.
Dawn was close now. I could hear him breathing,
I could hear him slowly breaking into
a smile... To think that this ghastly little

had actually bided his time! I agreed.
He set to work. At first, when he trembled
at the wheel, and started grinning, clutching
at the straws, just my luck, I thought,

this harmless creature's a cretin, a fool!
I watched myself in the window, growing
fainter by the minute. The white fields
glimmered. I couldn't look for long,

turning to see him suddenly transformed,
a living spirit, glistening, pure,
at the humming, spinning centre of the world,
where he struggled and played,

turning the difficult, flickering wisps –
as the first of the terrible sun
burst and broke in the room – into gold.
I'd never heard such laughter.

ii *The Messenger*

You should have seen her when I walked in.
Not yet fifteen, maid-in-waiting thin.
The king was not to be disturbed. Again.
We all knew what we weren't thinking.

By then, back from my third end of the earth
in a month, sick of rumours, crones' talk
and all that village-idiot breath,
I felt I'd far-flung myself enough.

I'd been wondering what to tell her,
weighing up the tallest stories –
set upon by harpies or queued to hear
a clairvoyant goat? – when I caught him

by his silhouette, deformed against the sun.
Poor bloke. When, I thought, was evil
ever this misshapen, out of luck?
Yet, as his small fire gathered in the dusk,

how lit and alive he looked, close up,
licked by the shadows, so much himself
he seemed for a second like anyone else
lost in the name of happiness.

I followed my reward. Next day,
she kept the court amused all morning,
watching the hopeful dance of his eyes
tremble on the tip of her tongue.

He was torn in two. At the final wrench
of his leaving, something crumpled in me
and I bowed, feeling the whole of my weight
in shame, not gold.

MY ALEXANDER

Golden boy. How I watched you
beautifully-limbed in my Ladybird book
stride among the cypresses,
your tutor's sad eyes following you too,

over the next few pages,
as far as your gorgeous breastplate, so striking
in battle, your braceleted arm
receiving the vanquished. To see you slice through

that knot, your muscles like that,
was where my book would always fall open.
Then the shining cities, flicked by,
knowing they'd lead to the last look from you,

your generals kneeling and weeping,
your pale, wounded head, dark women tending you.

FRENCH EXCHANGE

The first time I had anyone to miss
so of course I grasped at it,
keeping to my shuttered room,
sweat-shopping love-letters home
as promised. *Trust me*, I begged, long-distance.

Mealtimes, too, would bring on my sickness,
a too-rich sauce I couldn't keep down.
My head stuffed with hurt, my table talk
insisted on a gristly silence,
the host family mid-spoonful with concern.

Anything I felt had to be looked up, in case.
Their son knew more about England than I did.
Meanwhile, my diary gazed down on the days
pitiless and self-pitying,
bragging its beginner's Rousseau.

Sure enough, the abstract nouns I relied on –
solitude, angoisse, désespoir –
one by one proved *faux amis*. Most evenings,
I'd drift down to the local park
to hear the teenage girls meet up and kiss -

then sing the simplest things by heart.

THE RELIABLE NARRATOR c.1880

All morning, a modest fire leaps for his attention.
They should have been here by now! He begins to suspect.
Behind his back, his hands are more twisted
than a well-intentioned plot. Fated to misunderstand,
he doggedly paces the deep, sober carpet.
Coincidence stalks him. *In heaven's name!*

prefaces every inkling. Remarkable, isn't it,
how one runaway maid leads straight to his best friend
emphatically strangled? Or how his sash-windows
only ever overlook that shadowy figure
glimpsed through implausible fog. How, lately,
perfect strangers tell him far too much.

What can be keeping them? The most obvious clues
lie in the most ordinary objects
scattered wherever he settles to write
in that fervent tone he knows he'll never sustain.
He tries to think chapters ahead. *Surely someone saw –
or heard?* If he should try the door to the passageway now...

Out there, fat reflections of gaslight still smear
the cobblestones; his Lordship continues to ruin
his fortune and eyesight; in an echoing stairwell,
another pallid creature abandons herself
to unwise caresses; something goes on
prowling the towpaths, bent on the unspeakable.

LACE MOURNING FAN

Normandy 1857

It withers as it blooms,
its perfect etiquette
spreading out like some disease
or damaged chromosomes,
corrupt, yet intimate.

Its half-stifled fricatives
suggest an insect-wing,
unwieldy, looking for flight;
a blackened rattlesnake-skin
recoiling from the light.

At the salon, men admire
her nervous chic, and wait.
The latest widow-coquette:
where she goes, candlelight
weakens. But not yet, not yet.

MY SON, THE PRINCE OF BOHEMIA

'He's all my exercise, my mirth, my matter...
My parasite, my soldier, statesman, all.'
The Winter's Tale

A word, if I may, before he sees you.
I take it you've heard how he's grown,
how he sprawls all day in his luxury,
truffle-happy, tended only by those

who revere him, our lives in thrall
to the long vowel-sounds of his approval
or dismay. Lately, when he walks,
he walks amongst applause,

nosing out new dainties and distractions,
his eyes guzzling shine. As you might expect,
he's either raucously oblivious,
shaking off sleep like a flatterer's cloak,

or foxed by thoughts in which, it seems,
the fairground empties, flute music fades,
the travelling players pack up their things
in silence. Best avoided then.

Naturally, the boy's an absolute dissolute,
eager-earnest and amoral, all more and now,
with no time for meanwhiles in his head.
Say nothing of what you've been through,

the accumulation of ill-omens –
stormclouds threatening a knavish sea,
hairpin miles of neglected roadside wreaths,
the kingdom's entrails hung up for haruspicy.

Instead, the palace thrills to his commands:
every sound he makes is a proclamation.
By all means share in his certainties,
but be careful. There may be tantrums.

GOYA: THE 2ND OF MAY

Again and again, daggers draw our attention
to the pair of baggy, clownish pantaloons
whose backward somersault ends in tears.
The astonishing lengths he goes to! Death,
the acrobat, curves him like a scimitar.

Contortion reigns: the left foot one man
launches insurrection from is a size too large,
the arch triumphant and unbalancing.
He's actually toppling! At least one head's
been overturned already, facing Mecca.

Above it all, a ghostly sword of justice
hangs, hastily re-drawn. The sky is leaden,
dust. A blood-thin bell-tower warns the horizon.
Tomorrow the visiting troupes will no doubt
return, this time applying the rouge.

SEPTEMBER

Why wasn't my elder brother a sister?
She would've explained what girls were like.
Such as, how long did I have before I had to

have a girlfriend? In less than a week,
I'd be ten years old and starting my new school.
Another problematical autumn.

I already knew that daddy-long-legs
were really called crane flies. I knew that
three years ago. I used to catch them especially,

enjoying their whispers in my hands,
then gently unpick them. I laid the strands out
in silence. Short-lived, but mine. To be fair,

my mind must have been on other things,
as I let the ones I liked best clamber away
to the crazy-paving. Without warning,

my parents would loom up beyond the glass –
what was the matter? had I been crying? –
impossible to talk to. Without warning,

I'd think of when the rest of the class
would be working in silence, when, at last,
more impossible still, I'd be touching her fine,

straight hair, its warmth and unsuspecting hush.

SKETCHES BY PHIZ

Only Quilp persists. Fingerprint-distinct,
his grubby features whorled and gnarled, he humps
beside the rotting wharves to watch the tide
of his criminal Thames wash in: squat god;
river's spawn; indelible stain of ink.

Or else, entirely at his ease, he is
a gentleman of squalor, very much
chez lui, whose burgled charms and strangled vowels
disguise his whereabouts, hide his background.
He smokes a quiet pipe. In the distance,

sweltering, lie the chained and groaning Hulks.
He turns and grins, infectiously... His face
a creased and bunched tattoo, a printed fist,
with HATE stamped on the knuckles of his jaws,
he stands for everything I was taught to fear -

those sidelong intimations, those bad words
in my ear. Even now, his eyes – black dots –
burrow straight through me; he knows full well I'll
look away, and swear I didn't see him,
that I was nothing, no one, never there.

NOVEMBER SONG

after Baudelaire

Soon, we'll be plunged into freezing darkness –
forget all about that quick summer heat!
Gritters are already ploughing the slow lanes,
flashing their warning, scattering the gravel-seed.

The whole of winter's come back to me: bile,
sudden chills, outbursts, hatred and hard slog;
and, just like the sun in its Arctic hell,
I can feel my heart set in a red, icy block.

I flinch at the rock-salt spattering the screen,
as if gunned down by a rapid-fire of spite.
My mind is cracking up – a smithereens
of office space – after the explosive device.

Dust settles. Then the faintest pitter-patter
as if something somewhere's trapped behind glass.
But what? Summer's leapt to late November...
That odd sound again. Like some unnameable loss.

TOM CAT BECOMES A DAD

A screech of incredulous heels,
then klaxons. The full yikes of his eyes.
He braces as the anvil-words
come crashing down. Fatherhood.
Family. Real responsibility.

Inside him, a ragged xylophone
unravels. No more theme-tune.
His heart simply hammers away.
Again and again it hits him how
none of the usual effects can express

this feeling – or his fear of losing it.
From now on, each day will be laid out
like a badly-tended garden,
with every spade, rake and run-
away barrow just waiting to happen.

THE WRECK

Once you clamber out
and realize you're managing
fine, taking very small steps
one at a time, you can afford to
look back.

The black spill is getting worse,
everywhere. The thing still trembles,
still hisses, beseeches,
won't stop.
You can remember it now,

you can feel yourself starting to shake,
and your hands fly up, too late,
to snatch at the hard, horrible sound
you said you'd never make.

FAMOUS LAST WORDS

Charles Baudelaire 1821-1867

'She clung to a last few words which her son had been taught to pronounce.'

Lesson 1, unit 1. Now listen and repeat.
At the restaurant: the perfect table manners.
'Madame, passez-moi la moutarde, s'il vous plait.'

Charles is making progress, much to Mother's delight.
He soon toddles into language she remembers –
gaga, onomatopoeia, his calling out

for love and help in vain, learning it the hard way.
It's her chance to clean up his vocabulary;
expurgate his letters; invent new *contes de fées;*

re-biblicize, de-demonize him; make him say
he's sorry and wrong or she'll take his ABC
away from him and reintroduce the curé.

Charles is speechless with disease. A far, resigned
and silent cry from the dirty versifier,
dissident voice of rhymes so hammered and refined

they could unbalance alexandrines and your mind.
He goggles, open-mouthed, as if aphasia
were somehow just reward for having dared offend

state taste, criticize religion, his best work banned,
as if he really were their pervert and their liar,
as if they'd shut him up for good, or talked him round.

BYRON IN GREECE, 1810

Hobhouse recalls:

i

What would my mind
be like if I'd never known him?
What would my memories be worth?

I wish they could hold off the night,
or make it, too, go pale at the thought
of what he did when, and to whom, all those years ago.

I lie awake, by the half-open window,
retrieving. Mostly dust in my dreams now.
Better to wait till he comes back to me,

whole, out of the East,
just as he was before we all wronged him,
till the first faint scuffles of birdsong begin

and another risible English dawn sinks in.

ii

That winter, we had the ruins to ourselves.

There, in the most sacred places,
on cooling fragments, fluted stumps,
we felt their ache,
took to heart their hard instruction.

Their otherworldliness was ours.

We spent our sunsets thus,
lounging where the ancients sacrificed,
looking out at a country
coming darkly into leaf.

We probably saw too much.

By mid-March, I had made my notes,
my list of cautions, good advice.

Meanwhile, thunderous with boredom,
he'd be throwing stones at the mountains,
already gathering scorn.

Through all he said, his contrariness,
his silly self-regard, I could see
how women would want to love him,
would even save the flakes of his sunburnt skin -

keepsakes of what went on between them.

iii

Out on the plains
he can do no wrong.

There, amongst the thistles and stones,
he spurs his grey on

till at last he's no more than
a speck of self, a flawed and fleeting emblem

of recklessness – yet another gentleman
out riding his luck against the horizon.

Only this one's much more handsome.
Half of Athens knows all about him.

So what if he never wheels round?
His damnedest is already done.

That trying wind sent to rebuke him
can scarcely ruffle his calm.

In the shade of the one tree in blossom,
for once, no mood takes him.

He has no thoughts of home,
no thoughts at all of his own.

iv

How long past noon in the sticky, shuttered room
would he stay like that,
sprawled on his red and gold divan,
serenely at fault again?

From the balcony, I watched
as the best of the light came and went,
berating him,
until the whole, unforgettable prospect –
importunate Spring
at every grove and mountain stream –
appeared to look up for him in vain,
as if bursting to be described,
defined by him.

Later, when he saw how *I'd* put it…
His saying nothing…
Like that look he gave me,
after the rockfall in the gorge,
when the ground still shook
and I said we should go back.

v

We were the most penniless men in the world.
So what should we care?
For a long time, I was heavily,

happily indebted to him.
But our fortune couldn't last.
He'd be dissolute to prove a point.

At the squalid, overnight inn,
I wouldn't face what I kept hearing.
(You know how he fell on them –

like a locust in the corn,
all equally deserving,
his poor little things.)

I took a turn in the dark, wet yard
stumbling past the animals
lowing, and wondered when he'd be finished.

That night I dreamt about the boot-black
who couldn't shine enough,
the boy who blackened everything he touched.

'SPEAK. DEMAND. WE'LL ANSWER.'

One month in, there's only one mouth, and we end up
bent double, cackling and haggard,
the two of us stirring whenever he stirs.
Little toil and trouble.

By the looks of us, our thoughts have grown
borderline murderous,
as we watch ourselves, seeing the future
from the dark, narrow cave of our wonder.

COLERIDGE AT GRETA HALL

No more walks to find the source,
the stream that might recall her voice,
loving the little good it does.
A growing dependency on illness.

Sorrow's shape in everything.
An overdose of seeming.

How to explain this to his memories:
his mind, unsparing, on one commonplace –
steady rain as unremitting loss.

In his notebook, more and more misgivings,
his excuses more ingenious,
true love in code. The depths of metaphysics.

Sorrow's shape in everything.
An overdose of seeming.

Obsessive cloud-analysis
means no end of murmurs, glowers, sighs.
What's that rattling the storm-windows?
So many drops every two to three hours.

THE JUMP

'You what? Up there? Can you imagine it,
the spectacle you'd make, the timid, wet

splash of yourself, your awkward clatter
into the pool? And the ripples ever after?

Besides, you never learned to dive.' I'm right,
I know, knowing how I must look: desperate,

on the rungs, clinging to self-confidence.
One quick tug at my skimpy trunks

and I'm back to that girl in the swimsuit,
the cut and plunge of her all-at-first-sight,

her one-piece balancing act
the reason why I'm this far out.

The springboard trembles. Faced with sudden depth,
I'd like at least another breath,

to make my head come back to me.
Desire seems a long way down. Already,

I can taste the excuses. But one more step
and I fall in love, get the girl, grow up.

MY SON, THE PEARL DIVER

All around me, the deadpan sea-brilliance
as I count to another hundred. His first proper illness,

and I'm like an acting captain,
unmanned, self-mutinous, prowling my cabin,

giving myself orders no one would ever obey.
The sky bristles with dazzle: more untroubled blue

bringing yet more vigilance. Wonder,
I tell myself, is surely still worth waiting for,

so that when he comes back up,
when he shatters and gladdens the surface, sleep-

soaked and awkward,
I'm here to haul him aboard

and see the puzzled face I love
shine out, an unexpected trove.

ONLY A GAME

Abroad again. What could we do?... Bored,
on the steps of a white pavilion,
we gobbed. Huge drools of glittery spit
from the top of the iron rails

dribbed in separate pools. Nothing was held back.
That morning, we had argued with our parents;
we watched our venom froth and spasm
in the dust, totally absorbed...

When we next looked up, evening lined the sky.
Behind us, we could hear the click click click
of castanets: a dancing hall? Rude women?
We peeked and shuffled in. There, hushed, stretched

the glorious baize. Man's land. Where it seemed
you either sighed and muttered in the dark,
or had to hoard the light, accumulate,
wristy, self-assured. To us, of course,

the game was adult male and meaningless,
all talk of kisses and positioning.
Someone finished. The surface burned. It seemed
to call to us like perfect Wembley turf...

At last, here they come, the famous Boden brothers,
England's odds-on long-shot holders,
steadily holding their nerve. Watch them man-
handle those wobbly, toppling cues,

like whirling plate-jugglers without the plates!
Intent, as we were, on a backspin screw
with heavy side, right against the cushion,
we never heard the anguished owner's

stumbling rant that ended all our tiptoe
fun at once, in a single, vicious blow,
with heavy side. The white dot ball leapt
and bounced three times across the floor.

THE TOUCHLINE DADS

are trying hard to show more love,
to be bigger and better than yours.
Every Sunday, they prove themselves hoarse,
hurling encouragement, mouths full of

expertise and a strained affection.
They watch their boys in all weather
marking up and tackling back, getting further
and further stuck in. Only in time added on

do they begin to lose faith in them, handing down
the same hard-luck attitude
they themselves endured
as sons. No, not easily outgrown,

their own untold lack of ability,
their loss of cool
in front of goal,
the decisions that never went their way.

READING CALVINO'S *THE NON-EXISTENT KNIGHT* IN ITALIAN

The reader in shining armour, or so
I thought, myself as a real grail hero
plunging in the thick of words – no
dictionary to hand, no faithful Sancho –
rescuing meanings, watching each one grow
from the original's obscurest limbo
into limpid English, fluent prose. As though.

Instead, memory's overthrow,
the agonising, slow
breakdown in my vocab, the telltale, hollow
clunk of mental fatigue. Uh-oh:
here comes language's ultimate gauntlet throw,
another new verb's irregular, shuddering blow,
the defeated's shameful faceful. The echo

of retreat: I dunno, I dunno, I dunno.

THE SOUL'S PROGRESS TO HEAVEN

i

something scrawny riven dark
toiling into recognition
canvas rippling
oars in time
negotiating blue

ii

ingenious trireme
spectral shadow-timbered
mother ship
antique transport of sorrow and joy

iii

the final preparations
at the helm
an inscrutable figure
storm-scrawled and -spattered
going on

TWELFTH NIGHT, HULL

'O you are sick of self-love, Malvolio'

Slowly afterwards, whilst we chatter and steam
against the cold, stamping to be home,
his anger burns to an end. Who else
joined in? But the coach arrives to interrupt

our laughter, and as we pull away,
I notice hardly anyone sits together –
we've settled to remember him.
So what was it made him fear love's

comfort, all its difficult warmth?
He huddled his imaginings. Puffed out
and put upon, he stalked towards his fall,
as if suddenly sick of the long, outstanding

joke that's being played upon us all.
And although he deserved that bitter taste
of trouncing fate, I can still hear the wail
from his confessional, that cry behind

the grille. There's no reprieve; the show goes on.
And I must undergo my thoughts once more
where night's continuous industries flare
and chafe, as we cross the black river home.

THE STYLITES

Look at them, the high achievers,
up there still, steepling themselves against doubt.
Like self-made muezzins, their towering shouts

call us all to new ambition,
more success. And to be like them,
above all else. Their authority is

absolute, straight from the sun. All day long,
they describe our horizon, their shadows
lengthening over us. They have

all the humility of noon.
At night, they simply wrap themselves
more in themselves and think themselves

closer to God.

AT GAINSBOROUGH'S HOUSE

Cramped in a chair as unforgiving as age,
she hardly stirs, seeing the afternoons out.
No loss now, this time she gladly gives up,
devoted to her post, the past, to what
history's done to this one room upstairs.

No need either to look at the carefree
Abel Moysey M.P. in his fine air
and grace, nimbly-calved and smugly-buttoned,
as he flourishes his walking-stick at
somewhere like success, at a glowing dawn

whose jealous oils have long since yellowed, cracked.

MY SON, THE BOLLYWOOD STAR

You should see the eyes he makes
under the early-bird tree:
eyes that have learned
to lie in wait,
that love to listen,
the way a starlit prince
will stop to listen,
as he turns his back
on the palace
and steps lightly
out of the fairy-tale;
eyes that swallow
and follow
the darkness
wherever it goes
till it brightens in the drawn,
dawn face of the one
who loves him.
And when the light grows,
when it silvers
and flusters
the tree he basks beneath,
when the sunrise backcloth
welcomes the breeze,
he sighs,
and at the clack of his tongue,
he summons the hovering
consonants
and pours himself
into song.

DOUBLE SELF-PORTRAIT AS 12TH MAN AND SCORER

Not another summer Saturday
watching the second eleven
drowse to a draw again,
one of us ruefully replaying

a season's awful shot selection –
ambitious pulls, rash, wayward drives,
and a tendency to over-reach, mistime –
weighing what's left of his average

against those sticky afternoons
he could have been watching girls
at the local, outdoor swimming pool –
the warm, wet prints of their delicate feet

evaporating intimately –
filled with a longing to be anywhere
but here, stuck in this airless scorers' box,
with this other one's absolute pride

in his point-scoring blazer and tie,
and his unbroken attention-span,
the type who just has to be
first to the umpire's signal,

dotting in the dot balls
over after over,
like some assiduous, superior lover,
as if awaiting some ultimate test,

as if such faith and concentration
were reward enough, the right preparation.

WAR MOVIE (1.10 p.m. Channel 4)

The illness lifted, but still weak,
I'm stuck

with how the West should have won,
starring seven types of American:

the just, all-seeing Sarge,
mindful of the carnage

yet to come;
the rookie's painful over-enthusiasm;

his friend, the bookish one, clinging to facts,
until that close-up on his shattered specs;

the sneering, knowing rival
we just know will end up grateful;

let's not forget Tank,
the home- and girl-sick hunk

who never makes it back; the wise-guy,
still grinning, though it stopped being funny

months ago; and last, the coward who comes through,
the unlikely, giveaway hero

we're meant to recognize
from the start, watching him hurled white-eyed

in and out of self-belief, the final image
of him, there, at the rickety, miracle-bridge,

looking down on
his salvation,

blinking, stone-faced,
as if still unconvinced.

SNEAK

i

She has crept up on me,
four and three quarters,
bare-bottomed and knowing
she's not supposed to be,

counting on my reaction.
She has contained herself
this far,
padding through the kitchen

on purpose, thrilling
with deceit, the little mis-
chief-in-chief, the loper,
the all-manner-of -ling.

ii

She seems puzzled by
the understudy in the mirror,

as she tries out lines
she's overheard,

selves
she just thinks up.

She's invisible now
and tells me not to look,

tells me she's a
secret.

LEAVING THURROCK

i

Autumn's gone already.
You wish you could follow it so far south,
there'd be no such thing again.

ii

Not long left. Another walk like yesterday's
should do the trick: once round the sag
of worn industrial-belt – mostly glucose
and detergents now – suddenly gives way
to a view of overgrowth, gaunt Kent, and everywhere,
the look of last night's Thames.

iii

It's worst when you know you can't sleep.
Back you go to the window's black,
promising yourself. Meanwhile, all-night
river-fog; the deep, mournful calls
of the sea-going barges, narrowly
avoiding each other. More tension.
Then dawn over Basildon.

WEBS

We wake to find the spiders crowned
and gloating in the garden, fat with poise,
holding sway. Silken revolution. Only now
their intrigues come to light: the hostage air's
aghast with threads before you simply brush

them aside.

Since we're not talking any more,
you won't ever know, as you come back up
from the other side of the washing line,
that one spare peg held tight between your teeth,
how your hair has misted, pearled and braided,

like a bride's.

A MINOR FRENCH ROMANTIC

1 His eccentricities

This season, he's decided on Merino wool
for that finished, modish look. Beneath his tortured,
knitted brow, a surly necktie can say so much.

Since this is Paris, mid-July, he's sure to swoon
in all the right *salons*: the kind where clever, flustered
ladies rally round to soothe him with their touch.

How quickly he revives in Madame's silken rooms...
Sunday morning, he'll be out on his singular stroll,
down by the asphalt *quais*, heading for the boulevards,

a dozen muted skylarks leashed and gathered,
startling, in his fist.

2 His travels

Whether huffing through the heat-struck ruins
airily apart, or dwelling too long
in an ivy-cankered churchyard, prostrate

with the soul's concerns, he's always been true
to himself. There's been no escaping that.
Nothing, for him, but endless sigh-seeking...

No, better by far to be headed home,
lashed by a sudden, spectacular rain,
to be found, precariously pensive

on a cliff-top path, swishing at the bracken,
composing his farewell to love – again.
Yet on reflection, when the moonlight comes,

picking out the ragged sea-lace,
how ungainly seem the rock-formations:
all too easily he can imagine

that upturned paunch of his hauled in,
days later, by some local, idiot
fisherman. Another time, then. Besides,

he has a table, complete with starry,
panoramic views, set aside for one
at 'The Albatross', where by all accounts

the *moules marinière* are excellent.

3 His predilections

To be alone with his Turkish pipe,
idling nicely in the far-fetched or far-flung.

Outlandish laundry bills he wouldn't dream of
settling. Another six months' credit.

A rather fetching petulance. The English,
with their tartan and their vicious game of cricket.

Long deliberations at the brothel
over girls the same age as his daughters.

Anything, anything at the expense
of the bourgeoisie. Fireside laudanum.

Estaminet absinthe. The memory
of mother, silently unpinning her hair.

4 His ideal wife

Let him see... She shall be
nothing less than providential,
providential and young, most definitely
young (because youth was made for all men to admire)

practical, too, and game,
prompt to check the serving-girl's smile,
ruthlessly cool to his penniless friends,
a poised hostess at the new forte-piano.

So he sees her, one night,
descending an ornate staircase,
surprising him by taking his arm
and leading him to understand, beneath the stars,

how her dowry will be
also ample enough: she shall,
of course, have both the taste *and* the collection.
In time, she may even learn to forgive him.

5 His dealings with the poor

He knows what's required of people like him:
to seek unsullied Beauty everywhere,
even in the suburbs.

But back from his month-long pilgrimage
to hear the exiled, genial *maître*,
he wonders how

the old man manages to entertain
like that – such manifest joy
at the workhouse orphans' Nativity play –

when he himself can't quite bring himself
to touch them.

6 His tertiary syphilis

Further suppuration. Night-sweats in the knowledge
of certain paralysis, his organs failing him
one by one. He fears for his brain and keeps this fear
from no-one, his flippancy dissolved by tinctures
and an eager quack's dreadful coldwater 'cures'.
Worst of all, the search for a vein for the steady
self-injections. Ulcerous and blemished, he sinks
to the level of acceptance. No final trip,
after all, to the mineral spa, to doze
among the fashionable, his mind no longer on
more Schubert, nor the most tender of flirtations.

7 His legacy

Two doting, pious daughters
married into established families,
and a volume of shapely verse
in the manner of Lamartine
awaiting rescue from obscurity.

Part Two

At Vauxhall

A tour of the Gardens in their heyday

THE DIVESTMENT

Out of livery
and away from church early,
still feeling where the cuffs and collar rubbed,

he wades through the high corn,
down a path where he knows the big houses
can't see him. He could be anyone.

He has the green of the day ahead
and a saved shilling. And what now seems
opportune will soon be his by rights,

for this is the season.
Only Nature contests his happiness:
the larks' exorbitant warning-song;

bright rashes of foxgloves and rose-briars;
all the wide varieties of seed-heads
he can swish at with his stick.

At the river-crossing the gold wells up;
great cloud-stacks pride themselves
south, following his direction.

He has so many freedoms to consider.
All afternoon, God willing, he'll unlace
the white dress of luck at his leisure.

BALLOON FLIGHT

From slack, the silk
begins to pulse and stir,
to agitate for more, as though,
after several feints and a playful swoon,

what looks like show,
like bluster or false hope,
like someone wrestling with his soul,
could prove an inspiration, after all.

Or else, a threat -
the way a lurid drunk
instinctively rounds on the world,
daring us to look, as one of nightmare's

swollen creatures
is brought unnaturally
to term. Breathless with momentum,
it strains against its ropes, holding sway, till

the men get in
and set it free. We watch
it ripple up at last, past all
hyperbole, gathering so much speed

it simply tilts
the way we see ourselves,
our earthly possibilities.
Because it must mean something – something more

than a sign of
what remains beyond us –
before that cooling, wayward dot
just disappears, to leave us nothing but

each other's look
and much too much made clear:
that what's miraculous in May's
soon shrunk, become September's commonplace.

THE GRAND RE-OPENING

Returned to our preferences
and our senses, we fan out
into the familiar,
eager to unwind along
the same straight walks as before,
knowing the work's already
been done: beds made, lawns fresh-cut,

the whole accomplished backdrop
abruptly re-hung for us.
Since almost everything else
is, why can't *we* be ourselves
again? It's so good-natured
here, well-managed and clean. And
April re-touches us all,

helping us to recognise
the signs of a plausible
paradise, that other world
of measure, ease and latitude
in which, once, we simply moved
towards the forgiving light,
tilting into transgression.

MERMAN

An exile in his element,
he keeps himself hidden,
as if fearful of the real
Atlantic that's been poured into his tank
to make him feel
at home.

Every so often,
from behind the rocks,
unearthly song,
familiar sobs.

He won't come out for any coins
or promises,
won't sport for us at all.

When all we want is to see the join.

Having paid, haven't we the right
to a handful of stones,
to hurl whatever comes to mind?

At least, until the great tail stills.

UNDERGROUND SAINT

One only at a time,
though there's never any queue:
some peculiar taint in the air –
penitence, perhaps,
or salt self-preservation.

Lickable wet down the grotto walls;
the crunch of oyster-shells underfoot;
a single, lit candle-stub
gulping at shadows:
this way to the alcove.

Fragile exhibit
roped off from the gloom,
he holds himself apart,
his holiness mostly
bones and breathlessness.

You may approach him of course –
hard as icon.
No marks, no signs,
not a single proof on him.
No chance of souvenirs.

THE RADICAL

Never scandalous enough, the scandals
still follow him, his little circle
tutting and tightening against him,

his own kind. Well, if that's what they want,
he'll bide his time on the continent.
There are strings of cloud threading east right now.

All the government men are watching his ideas.
Insights in the main and fulminations
for when the wind truly gets up.

Even here, where the ailing evening listens in,
where all the couples in luck look straight past him,
trouble still carries: the repeated dinnings

of an imagined city in foment,
the final throes of the well-sponsored bells,
one last steeple going up in the sun,

the hush and roar of New Tyburn.

A MIDSUMMER FIRE

Scant light
before a worse cloud threatens.
Misalliance amongst the nations.
Time to bring everything in.

Across the gravelled walk, a kitchen-hand
is dragging a scuttle two-handed,
doggedly scouring a path,
as it catches, catches, catches his heels.

THE TRUE PATH

On all fours, bowed by visions
and his need to see more of them,
he undergoes his punishment,
round and round the perimeter walk,
performing his expiation.

Good dog, knowing what wills him on
has willed no end to his penance,
his gruff volition.
He must simply keep to the edges,
keep his sunburnt scruff in the sun.

For charity, he will bare the black teeth
of his bark, hold out his bandaged hands
and point to the stumps of his bandaged feet,
to where the rainbow-sepsis runs,
true token of his humility.

Though he stinks of sin and other,
underlying things, his scuffed eyes shine
when he describes, as though mapped from above,
Jerusalem, the night he walked beside
the king of kings...

Disbelieve him and he'll retreat
to a low growl, remembering
the pain and contrition he's in,
knowing full well what the other
can do to him, the stranger and

the master.

THE NATURAL HEIR

Mid-afternoon
insouciance
leads to nothing less

than a light, pleasurable nap.
Rich, permissible dreams
in which he renews

some old acquaintance
more persuasively than before...
Snug as a banked fire,

he sits in full sun
beneath the lilac,
life inexplicably become

a succession of lulls,
flashes of a notional heaven,
thoughts of the heydays to come.

Nothing new
on his conscience now,
but upkeep and inducements,

improving yields
at the plantation.
After a while, some refreshment.

Most diverting,
the way the just world
wheels around him, considerate,

minding its splendour,
the earnest and the virtuous,
for just a little longer,

enjoying their allowance.

WISHFUL PICKING

There are scrapes
he'd gladly get into again

if only
to get his hands on

some of that
irresistible black,

still hanging,
forbidden and

sweet,
just out of reach.

And afterwards,
to know no hiding –

to show his tell-tale hands
and lips.

ILLUSTRATED MAN

Creatures from the seven seas
ride him back to front.
Unreadable now,
the names of those he's lost.

Ripples of mermaids,
blurred monsters from the deep.
They make him strip
to sing the tall-tale shanty of his skin.

At night, under the tilting stars,
he climbs the sad, blue rigging
of his memories,
twitches in his far-off sleep.

FORTUNE-TELLER

Having seen into the summer
and guessed the rest,
he's not best pleased:
nothing for it for the dreamer

and his dreamy son and daughter
than to dream again.
So let worse happen.
No fault of his if it's there in the future.

AN EXAMPLE

A little strange, it's true.

Take that mad fellow there,
frantically at whatever he's got,
in the portico, there in the sun –
for all his colourful noises,
his hostile gestures at the air,
he most likely means no harm,
means nothing at all.

I don't think so.

No, what he's counting off on his fingers
will either be blessings or lessons –
or maybe some pittance he can't quite believe in.
Plain enough how much it hurts -
look how he puts his hands to his head
and starts pulling at the stings.

Oh, some dissipation or other.
They say he's an actuary
brought low by the very law he practises,
by forces he couldn't foresee,
or by some fashionable disease.

No, God sees to him.

I take it you've seen our Great Wheel.

Once, when he started in on them
with his predicament,
I saw a whole family
get to its feet
and set its children onto him.

As I said, these are our customs.

SONNETTE

Upon the hour, the clock performs:
to the charming strains of a minuet,
pairs of red-cheeked, porcelain lovers –

the well-tuned *bienheureux* – duly appear
to bend and pirouette towards each other,
interlocking minute hands and minute

lips, trembling with one intention –
to meet in an exquisite, timely kiss,
knowing each must part and then make way for

that single, smiling figurine
whose every dainty, downward stroke
means well, but only measures out

the silence.

THE MAZE

'It's this way,'
says her husband,
but she finds it's not.

THE STATUE OF DIANA

White marvel.
Skin so even.
Admirably done.
The mute appeal
of all
we're meant
to gaze upon.

Full-length
silence.
Her seeled eyes
spare no one:
perfect contempt
for both the captain
and his men.

THE ENGLISH DISEASE

The obligations of spring:
find him somewhere quiet
to still his hands.

There's a clearing he knows
where time at least
will leave him alone.

Should've known better.
Scraps of an old song.
Same troublesome cough.
No quarter ever.

Blurring under him,
her eyes look like they've lost
their place in a page
she'd meant to get by heart.

Strange music.
The sudden curl
of his tongue –
like a lyre –
in her mouth.

By the sunken pool
she readily admits
things she never did.
Now they can go home.

In the long walk,
in the dark,
anyone can make a mistake,
let him make his mark.

This little petard
likes to make a lot of noise
before it sputters out.

Silence
as she counts the stars,
imagining the distance.

He finishes off
the plate of whelks
in some discomfort.

He says he'll teach her her letters.
The illegible scrawl of her skirts
perplexes him.

His little row of oh oh ohs
as she steadies his hand
and corrects him.

Behind her head
the rising strains
of – isn't that? –
Haydn?

THE INCOMPLETE DESIGN

He kept it from her, in a rosewood drawer,
as though ashamed of his uncertainty:
what had started out as an ideal bridge
between two eagerly-realized shores

leapt into detail: the flush, coloured squares
of sun-warmed sandstone, tender, fruiting swags
and a sweeping balustrade that promised
so much more, indefinitely. For days,

a measured arc of dots had soared towards
the first projected span, already outlined
and willing, until his hand had faltered,
his vision shying at sheer predicament,

the curve become implausible and wrong,
held up in airy guesswork, in baffled,
pencilled gestures scrabbling for a foothold
far above a scrawl of fainter shading,

intending the abyss.

THE CHASTENING

A new plain-speaking:
she's not where she said she'd be.
Reckless fog and his own timidity
have seen to that.

He watches his breath catch up with him -
swirls of the worst surmises;
then catches a gust of laughter ghosting off,
unmistakably not hers.

Wet will get everywhere;
in his face, his shrivelled stockings,
his ruined gloves and hair.
And the turning trees can please themselves.

He must go back the way he came,
back across the neat parterres,
the displays, the bold arrangements,
back to the dry of the summerhouse,

back to all the others. Now and then,
a spluttering bird, fearful and indignant.
Two visitors stop to wonder
at him, then carry on in German.

Gradually, lines of potted palms
emerge, like supplicants, their hostage fronds
bound hard for winter. Statues, too,
are being boxed in,

frangible heroes braced for the dark,
sword-arms raised against the coming frosts.

THE DRINKER

Last orders among the lower orders –
his lowest spirits yet.
The red-faced hostess

will only offer him a sip
from a bottle of home-made 'serious stuff',
a viscous plum murk,

the colour of heartsick heart's blood,
discolouring as she speaks.
Elixir, she calls it.

It will cost what he has.

Smoke grasps at the opened mouth.

All he has now is his unquenchable youth.

SHUT IN

Why does it always happen
that the best day of the season
turns in on itself so soon,
as if waiting for some resolution?

And why does the ironwork on that gate
look so wrought?
Surely these late strands of light
can tease a right way out?

THE DEBTOR

Sheltering under a spindly ash,
he leans back and watches the bailiffs
come for him, this time, sure of him,
taking their time. Quarry,
like his father before him,
the whole unwholesome inheritance.

As ever, summer's in arrears;
the first demeaning spots of rain
from a disobliging June.
The evening's greyish tinge steals in.

Though dressed for the occasion
in a sumptuous, rich pea-green,
he stands there shivering,
unable to blend in.

That rumpled goddess on her plinth
would surely pity him
if she hadn't already turned
her supplicant's eyes to heaven.

A pigeon thrashes through the canopy,
presaging some unseemliness,
some final scuffle.

And whenever the wind drops,
a woodpecker's fervent tocks
sound like bone-dice in a cup.

At a remove, the relieving tumble
of the New Cascade, installed this summer,
at great cost. Above it, he can just make out,
as advertised, the guest soprano's
wobbly *sostenuto* draw out the applause,
a rapture made more genteel by distance.

He ought to empty his pockets,
for now, at a signal, the men begin to cut
across the lawn's hypoteneuse,
breaking all the rules
in a barely precipitate walk.

THE DREAM OF THE WATCH

In which the night-light trembles of its own accord.
Over his shoulder, gathering mysteries:
the night-air, drowsy with promises, moth-furred,
filled with the heaven-sent of untold mistresses.

AMONG THE SONGBIRDS

But one of them won't. Unsurprised
by circumstance, he puzzles at
his feathers with the thoroughness
of one enjoying finding fault.

Unthinking almost all the time,
he keeps his head down and soon dis-
colours. *One day*, the others chorus,
the cage will open. Like a mind.

THE WOULD-BE SUICIDE

Bested again,
he picked the tree
for its 'very dark leaves'
that wouldn't dance in wind or rain.

He knew the shadow it cast
would, for someone, be most bewildering
later that evening –
and vast.

That end never came.
He just stood
where the white blossom
had carried

(and dropped).

LIGHT GOES

A little less and
it will feel like autumn's won.

Hardly anyone is sitting out.
That episode is over.

Besides, who's left
to see him take advantage?

Remember his dark advances,
a little lesson.

COMEBACK

How much higher?
He knows we won't be satisfied
till he sets himself on fire.

No matter what,
he'll climb the back of the night tonight
to get inside our memories,

get to our applause.
He will be seen; he will be heard;
borne up by our hurrahs.

Man of squibs, man of stars,
in a suit of brilliant gauze,
tonight he'll wear his famous

pained white face and allow himself to fall,
burning like an answered prayer,
or revelation, a final,

dying word.

THE VERDICT

The caged birds know all about us;
no longer in danger, they're free
to study us at our leisure,

the way we like to take our time,
take such complicated trouble
with each other, feinting and deigning,

intimating love - or its like -
in a glut of looks and gestures,
from every well-meant bound-to-be,

first flush to late luxuriance -
or a glassy-eyed decorum
no one ever dreamed of.

No one listens to the discreet,
unflustered chorus from above,
though the evening air warms to its tune.

How shrill we sound, how glazed we look
remains a matter of opinion;
less so, how we missed our chance of

lasting pleasure far too easily...
Oblivious, the birds sing on...
What, then, does it say about us,

that moment when the gates are locked
and the last hoarse shout's quite snuffed out,
that they should all fall silent?

Have a look at our website for more lovely books

www.redhandbooks.co.uk

www.ingramcontent.com/pod-product-compliance
Ingram Content Group UK Ltd.
Pitfield, Milton Keynes, MK11 3LW, UK
UKHW020420250726
13967UKWH00007B/2739